# Holy Beautiful Contemplation

Lectio and Visio Divina For A Holy and
Beautiful Life

Holy Beautiful Contemplation

# Table of Contents:

# What is Lectio Divina?

Lectio Divina is a contemplative way of reading the Bible. It dates to the early centuries of the Christian Church and was established as a monastic practice by Benedict in the 6th century. It is a way of praying the scriptures that leads us deeper into God's word. We slow down. We read a short passage more than once. We reflect on it. We savor it. We learn from it. We embrace it.

A HOLY AND BEAUTIFUL GOD SEES ME, HEARS ME, AND GUIDES ME.

When we slow down and listen, God begins to speak to us in a new way. The words speak to us personally and grows that union we have with God through Christ who is Himself the Living and Breathing Word. Amen.

Thomas Cranmer in his Homily on Scripture ended it with an exhortation to read it in this way: "Let us ruminate, and, as it were, chew the cud, that we may have the sweet juice, spiritual effect, marrow, honey, kernel, taste, comfort and consolation of them." Fr Christopher Jamison, former Abbot of Worth Abbey in Sussex, England, in his book *Finding Sanctuary* writes of three key features of lectio:
· The first is that "the text is seen as a gift to be received, not a problem to be dissected…. let the text come to you."
· The second is that the lectio tradition "teaches us that in order to receive what the text has to offer we must read slowly."
· The third is that lectio is "a way of prayer. Before reading pray that God will speak to you through the text. During reading, allow the reading to evolve into meditation and then into prayer and finally contemplation. When the reading is concluded, keep some phrase in mind and repeat tit throughout the day so that prayerful reading becomes prayerful living."

So, Lectio Divina is not Bible study but something beautifully different. The practice understands Scripture as a meeting place for a personal encounter with a Holy and Beautiful God. It is a practice we come to with the desire to be changed at all sorts of levels. It defines us on a much more emotional level.

Through it we allow ourselves to be formed in the likeness of Christ. Through it we find sacred tools for a sacred space. Doing things with intention and reverence brings depth and daily focus.
It is another tool to learn to live a more holy and beautiful life.

# "First of all, every time you begin a good work, you must pray to Him most earnestly to bring it to perfection."

Rule of St Benedict, Prologue

# How to Use This Book

*Lectio Divina* is a practice of listening with the ears of our heart to a short passage of Scripture. It allows for an opening to the Spirit speaking to us directly and specifically. It is a contemplative practice because it positions us to encounter God and be encountered by God. There are four movements in Lectio Divina. You will need a journal/paper, pen or pencil, and a Bible. You can also play music in the background and light some candles. We encourage you to create a sacred space to encounter the divine.

How to practice Lectio Divina:

*Read (Lectio):* Read the passage through slowly and contemplatively. Listen for the word or the phrase that is addressed to you. Write it down or circle it.

*Reflect (Meditatio):* Read the passage again, slowly, and meditatively. Listen for where this word or phrase connects with your life. Ask, "What in my life needs to hear this word or phrase?" "How is my life touched by this word or phrase?" Write down your real and honest thoughts.

*Respond (Oratio):* Read the passage a third time, slowly and thoughtfully, listening for your own deepest and truest response. Allow a natural conversation with God to flow from your engagement with this passage and its personal meaning. Contemplate, "What is my response to God based on what I have read and heard from the Spirit?" Write it down.

*Rest (Contemplatio):* Read the text one final time, resting in God, yielding to Him, and savoring what you have received.

*Resolve (Incarnatio):* As you come to the end of your time, resolve to carry this word into the context of your life today. Keep listening for deeper insight and understanding. Treasure the gift that God has given and watch for ways in which God continues to speak.

At the end of each month, you will also find a *Visio Divina*, a practice known as praying with our eyes.

Visio Divina is another way to be contemplative. Visio Divina shares roots with the ancient practice of Lectio Divina.

Lectio Divina calls for a slow, careful interaction with scripture through meditation and prayer, allowing a word or phrase to rise in one's consciousness, a holy and beautiful word to be savored and examined. Similarly, Visio Divina invites one to encounter God through images.

There are four basic steps to help start the practice of **Visio Divina:**

- Read through a short passage of scripture or choose a verse, then be still. Settle into a comfortable posture to listen to God's voice.

- Meditate. Ponder the words, then gaze, look, observe, ask questions, and ask God to help you see what He wants you to see or what He wants you to notice. What stirs within you? What do you think is holy? What do you find beautiful?

- Pray. Pray through the text or what you notice in the image. Ask God for His help.

- Contemplate. We live the text. A contemplative spiritual exercise is meant to lead us to gospel action in the world and deeper, more intimate connection with God. It allows us to not only see the holy and beautiful but to let it become part of us so we can reveal it to others.

Our recommendation is to pair your Visio Divina with a passage of scripture when possible. Doing so opens the possibility of "deeper engagement with the Word" as Juliet Benner writes in her excellent book *Contemplative Vision: A Guide to Christian Art and Prayer.* She says, "We are blind to God's presence in the midst of our lives, we are unable to see where and how God is working to transform us and the world." Visio Divina helps us connect to God and notice where He is present in our lives.

In addition, you can add:

- What caught your eye? What do you notice? How does it make you feel?

- Reflect on the structure: color, lines, shadows, values, intensity.

- What is the mood of the painting?

- How do you react to it?

- Do you sense an invitation from God?

- What did you learn about God's nature and character?

- What strikes you as holy? Where do you see beauty?

How might you respond to God in prayer today? Does thanksgiving and gratitude well up in you? Or do the difficulties of this season you are currently in weigh you down? If so, sit a while longer with the image. Biblical meditation provokes honest thoughts, questions, and hopeful conversation with God. It is a holy and beautiful place where we speak and a place to be silent and listen to the voice of our Shepherd. Perhaps the best response is to be still and aware of His love for you.

**What would it be like if you lived each day, each breath, as a work of art in progress? Imagine that you are a Masterpiece unfolding every second of every day, a work of art taking form with every breath.**
**—Thomas Crum**

## There is a Season for Everything | Ecclesiastes 3:11

*Father let me hear from you. Fill my heart, soul, and mind with your presence and discernment from your Holy Spirit. Let your words be a living water quenching my thirst for your goodness.*

### Intro to the Scripture

The theme found in Ecclesiastes is the necessity of fearing God in a broken world. We all seek to understand the ways God is moving in this world, but we cannot because we are not God, yet we do not despair. As faithful children of God, we cling to Him even when we do not understand what He is doing. In Ecclesiastes, we find true wisdom: understanding what it means to truly fear God and His commandments.

# REMEMBER:

**Read** slowly and prayerfully /Lectio (Read)

**Reflect** /Meditatio (Focus on a word or phrase/listen)

**Respond**/ Oratio (Pray to God)

**Rest**/Contemplate/ Contemplatio (Rest in God)

**Resolve**/Incarnatio (Carry this Word in your life)

Sit quietly for a moment. Take a deep breath in and release. Allow His presence to wash over you.

Begin.

# Lectio Divina Day One

**Ecclesiastes 3:11** (AMP)

He has made everything beautiful *and* appropriate in its time. He has also planted eternity [a sense of divine purpose] in the human heart [a mysterious longing which nothing under the sun can satisfy, except God]— yet man cannot find out (comprehend, grasp) what God has done (His overall plan) from the beginning to the end.

**Soul Exploration:**

1. What word or phrase settled within your heart? In silence, meditate on that.

2. What is Christ's call to you through the word or phrase?

3. What wisdom did He give you? How will you integrate it into your current circumstances this week?

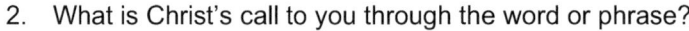

# Lectio Divina Day Two

**Ecclesiastes 3:11 (HCSB)** He has made everything appropriate in its time. He has also put eternity in their hearts, but man cannot discover the work God has done from beginning to end.

**Soul Exploration:**

1. What word or phrase settled within your heart? In silence, meditate on that.

2. What is Christ's call to you through the word or phrase?

3. What wisdom did He give you? How will you integrate it into your current circumstances this week?

# Lectio Divina Day Three

**Ecclesiastes 3:11 (NKJV)** He has made everything beautiful in its time. Also, He has put eternity in their hearts, except that no one can find out the work that God does from beginning to end.

**Soul Exploration:**

1.  What word or phrase settled within your heart? In silence, meditate on that.

2.  What is Christ's call to you through the word or phrase?

3.  What wisdom did He give you? How will you integrate it into your current circumstances this week?

# Lectio Divina Day Four

**Ecclesiastes 3:11 (VOICE**) *and I know* God has made everything beautiful for its time. God has also placed in our minds a sense of eternity; we look back on the past and ponder over the future, yet we cannot understand the doings of God.

**Soul Exploration:**

1. What word or phrase settled within your heart? In silence, meditate on that.

2. What is Christ's call to you through the word or phrase?

3. What wisdom did He give you? How will you integrate it into your current circumstances this week?

# Lectio Divina Day Five

**Ecclesiastes 3:11 (NRSVCE)** He has made everything suitable for its time; moreover, he has put a sense of past and future into their minds, yet they cannot find out what God has done from the beginning to the end.

**Soul Exploration:**

1. What word or phrase settled within your heart? In silence, meditate on that.

2. What is Christ's call to you through the word or phrase?

3. What wisdom did He give you? How will you integrate it into your current circumstances this week?

# Lectio Divina Day Six

**Ecclesiastes 3:11 (CEV)** God makes everything happen at the right time. Yet none of us can ever fully understand all he has done, and he puts questions in our minds about the past and the future.

**Soul Exploration:**

1. What word or phrase settled within your heart? In silence, meditate on that.

2. What is Christ's call to you through the word or phrase?

3. What wisdom did He give you? How will you integrate it into your current circumstances this week?

# Lectio Divina Day Seven

**Ecclesiastes 3:11 (YLT)** The whole He hath made beautiful in its season; also, that knowledge He hath put in their heart without which man findeth not out the work that God hath done from the beginning even unto the end.

**Soul Exploration:**

1.  What word or phrase settled within your heart? In silence, meditate on that.

2.  What is Christ's call to you through the word or phrase?

3.  What wisdom did He give you? How will you integrate it into your current circumstances this week?

# Weekly Sacred Examen

## A Weekly Reflection

St. Ignatius Loyola's Examen is an opportunity for peaceful reflective prayer. It invites us to find the movement of God in all the people and events of our life. The Examen is simply a set of introspective prompts for you to follow or adapt to your own character and spirit.

Begin with a pause and a slow, deep breath or two; become aware that you are in the presence of a Holy and Beautiful God.

## Thanksgiving

What am I especially grateful for in the past week? (The gift of another day...The love and support I have received...Something I have enjoyed….A moment I felt God's presence…..)

## Petition

I am about to reflect upon my week of Lectio Divina, I ask for the wisdom to know God and to know myself as God sees me.

## Review

What did I learn in the Scriptures I read?

Where did I experience joy?

What troubled me?

What challenged me?

Did I pause and find Selah?

What was something beautiful or holy that was revealed to me?

## Response

In response to this examen of my life, how have I grown my faith? How did I cultivate a place of joy and rest? What did God teach me in His Word?

## A Look Forward

As I look forward, what comes to mind?

How do I want to enter tomorrow? How will I cultivate peace in my life?

### Fall in Love | Ephesians 1:4

*Father let me hear from you. Fill my heart, soul, and mind with your presence and discernment from your Holy Spirit. Let your words be a living water quenching my thirst for your goodness.*

### Intro to the Scripture

There are three main themes of Ephesians: (1) Christ has reconciled all creation to Himself and to God; (2) Christ has united people from all nations to Himself and to one another in His church; and (3) Christians must live as new people.

Ephesians offers general instruction in the truths of God's redemptive work in Christ; the unity of the church among diverse peoples; and proper conduct in the church, the home, and the world.

# REMEMBER:

**Read** slowly and prayerfully /Lectio (Read)

**Reflect** /Meditatio (Focus on a word or phrase/listen)

**Respond**/ Oratio (Pray to God)

**Rest**/Contemplate/ Contemplatio (Rest in God)

**Resolve**/Incarnatio (Carry this Word in your life)

Sit quietly for a moment. Take a deep breath in and release. Allow His presence to wash over you.

Begin.

# Lectio Divina Day One

**Ephesians 1:4 (TPT)** Because of His great love, he ordained us, so that we would be seen as holy in his eyes with an unstained innocence.

**Soul Exploration:**

1. Do you see yourself as holy and beautiful in God's eyes?

2. What is Christ's call to you through this scripture?

3. What wisdom did He give you? How do you see yourself now? Has He removed something?

# Lectio Divina Day Two

**Ephesians 1:4** (NIV) For he chose us in him before the creation of the world to be holy and blameless in his sight. In love.

**Soul Exploration:**

1. Do you see yourself as holy and beautiful in God's eyes?

2. What is Christ's call to you through this scripture?

3. What wisdom did He give you? How do you see yourself now? Has He removed something?

# Lectio Divina Day Three

**Ephesians 1:4 (NLT)** Even before he made the world, God loved us and chose us in Christ to be holy and without fault in his eyes.

**Soul Exploration:**

1. Do you see yourself as holy and beautiful in God's eyes?

2. What is Christ's call to you through this scripture?

3. What wisdom did He give you? How do you see yourself now? Has He removed something?

# Lectio Divina Day Four

**Ephesians 1:4 (ESV)** Even as he chose us in him before the foundation of the world, that we should be holy and blameless before him. In love.

**Soul Exploration:**

1. Do you see yourself as holy and beautiful in God's eyes?

2. What is Christ's call to you through this scripture?

3. What wisdom did He give you? How do you see yourself now? Has He removed something?

# Lectio Divina Day Five

**Ephesians 1:4 (KJV)** According as he hath chosen us in him before the foundation of the world, that we should be holy and without blame before him in love.

**Soul Exploration:**

1.  Do you see yourself as holy and beautiful in God's eyes?

2.  What is Christ's call to you through this scripture?

3.  What wisdom did He give you? How do you see yourself now? Has He removed something?

# Lectio Divina Day Six

**Ephesians 1:4 (GNT)** Even before the world was made, God had already chosen us to be his through our union with Christ, so that we would be holy and without fault before him. Because of his love.

**Soul Exploration:**

1. Do you see yourself as holy and beautiful in God's eyes?

2. What is Christ's call to you through this scripture?

3. What wisdom did He give you? How do you see yourself now? Has He removed something?

# Lectio Divina Day Seven

**Ephesians 1:4 (CEV)** Before the world was created, God had Christ choose us to live with him and to be his holy and innocent and loving people.

**Soul Exploration:**

1. Do you see yourself as holy and beautiful in God's eyes?

2. What is Christ's call to you through this scripture?

3. What wisdom did He give you? How do you see yourself now? Has He removed something?

# Weekly Sacred Examen

## A Weekly Reflection

St. Ignatius Loyola's Examen is an opportunity for peaceful reflective prayer. It invites us to find the movement of God in all the people and events of our life. The Examen is simply a set of introspective prompts for you to follow or adapt to your own character and spirit.

Begin with a pause and a slow, deep breath or two; become aware that you are in the presence of a Holy and Beautiful God.

## Thanksgiving

What am I especially grateful for in the past week? (The gift of another day...The love and support I have received...Something I have enjoyed....A moment I felt God's presence.....)

## Petition

I am about to reflect upon my week of Lectio Divina. I ask for the wisdom to know God and to know myself as God sees me.

## Review

What did I learn in the Scriptures I read?

Where did I experience joy?

What troubled me?

What challenged me?

Did I pause and find Selah?

What was something beautiful or holy that was revealed to me?

## Response

In response to this examen of my life, how have I grown my faith? How did I cultivate a place of joy and rest? What did God teach me in His Word?

## A Look Forward

As I look forward, what comes to mind?

How do I want to enter tomorrow? How will I cultivate peace in my life?

# He is Plentiful | Luke 10:2

*Father let me hear from you. Fill my heart, soul, and mind with your presence and discernment from your Holy Spirit. Let your words be a living water quenching my thirst for your goodness.*

## Intro to the Scripture

Here are a few thoughts that may be able to expand our view the next time we think of Jesus' sending out workers into the harvest:

**Luke 10:1-12 seems to present entire worlds—or Kingdoms—crashing together.** The Kingdom of God and the Kingdom of this World.

**There are definite characteristics of God's Kingdom—a Kingdom that is described as having "come near" in verse 11.** And what characteristics does this Kingdom exhibit? One is **peace.** Another is **healing.** And that healing touches both physical and spiritual dimensions. Specifically, Jesus says to heal the sick, which presents a picture of wholeness or shalom. In fact, the Hebrew word for peace is *shalom*, which goes far beyond the absence of conflict.

Looking around the globe today we see many examples of hostility, injustice, and lack of love. The gospel challenges us to be messengers of peace.

## REMEMBER:

**Read** slowly and prayerfully /Lectio (Read)

**Reflect** /Meditatio (Focus on a word or phrase/listen)

**Respond**/ Oratio (Pray to God)

**Rest**/Contemplate/ Contemplatio (Rest in God)

**Resolve**/Incarnatio (Carry this Word in your life)

Sit quietly for a moment. Take a deep breath in and release. Allow His presence to wash over you.

Begin.

# Lectio Divina Day One

**Luke 10:2 (ESV)** And he said to them, "The harvest is plentiful, but the laborers are few. Therefore, pray earnestly to the Lord of the harvest to send out laborers into his harvest.

**Soul Exploration:**

1. Do you see yourself as holy and beautiful in God's eyes?

2. What is Christ's call to you through this scripture?

3. What wisdom did He give you? How do you see yourself now? Has He removed something?

# Lectio Divina Day Two

**Luke 10:2 (NIV)** He told them, "The harvest is plentiful, but the workers are few. Ask the Lord of the harvest, therefore, to send out workers into his harvest field.

**Soul Exploration:**

1. Do you see yourself as holy and beautiful in God's eyes?

2. What is Christ's call to you through this scripture?

3. What wisdom did He give you? How do you see yourself now? Has He removed something?

# Lectio Divina Day Three

**Luke 10:2 (ASV)** And he said unto them, the harvest indeed is plenteous, but the laborers are few: pray ye therefore the Lord of the harvest, that he send forth laborers into his harvest.

**Soul Exploration:**

1. Do you see yourself as holy and beautiful in God's eyes?

2. What is Christ's call to you through this scripture?

3. What wisdom did He give you? How do you see yourself now? Has He removed something?

# Lectio Divina Day Four

**Luke 10:2 (KJV)** Therefore said he unto them, The harvest truly is great, but the labourers are few: pray ye therefore the Lord of the harvest, that he would send forth labourers into his harvest.

**Soul Exploration:**

1.  Do you see yourself as holy and beautiful in God's eyes?

2.  What is Christ's call to you through this scripture?

3.  What wisdom did He give you? How do you see yourself now? Has He removed something?

# Lectio Divina Day Five

**Luke 10:2 (MSG)** He gave them this charge: What a huge harvest! And how few the harvest hands. So, on your knees, ask the God of the Harvest to send harvest hands.

**Soul Exploration:**

1. Do you see yourself as holy and beautiful in God's eyes?

2. What is Christ's call to you through this scripture?

3. What wisdom did He give you? How do you see yourself now? Has He removed something?

# Lectio Divina Day Six

**Luke 10:2 (NAS)** And He was saying to them, "The harvest is plentiful, but the laborers are few; therefore, beseech the Lord of the harvest to send out laborers into His harvest.

**Soul Exploration:**

1. Do you see yourself as holy and beautiful in God's eyes?

2. What is Christ's call to you through this scripture?

3. What wisdom did He give you? How do you see yourself now? Has He removed something?

# Lectio Divina Day Seven

**Luke 10:2 (TPT)** [He] released them with these instructions: "The harvest is huge and ripe. But there are not enough harvesters to bring it all in. As you go, plead with the Owner of the Harvest to drive out[a] into his harvest fields many more workers.

**Soul Exploration:**

1. Do you see yourself as holy and beautiful in God's eyes?

2. What is Christ's call to you through this scripture?

3. What wisdom did He give you? How do you see yourself now? Has He removed something?

# Weekly Sacred Examen

## A Weekly Reflection

St. Ignatius Loyola's Examen is an opportunity for peaceful reflective prayer. It invites us to find the movement of God in all the people and events of our life. The Examen is simply a set of introspective prompts for you to follow or adapt to your own character and spirit.

Begin with a pause and a slow, deep breath or two; become aware that you are in the presence of a Holy and Beautiful God.

## Thanksgiving

What am I especially grateful for in the past week? (The gift of another day...The love and support I have received...Something I have enjoyed….A moment I felt God's presence…..)

## Petition

I am about to reflect upon my week of Lectio Divina. I ask for the wisdom to know God and to know myself as God sees me.

## Review

What did I learn in the Scriptures I read?

Where did I experience joy?

What troubled me?

What challenged me?

Did I pause and find Selah?

What was something beautiful or holy that was revealed to me?

**Response**

In response to this examen of my life, how have I grown my faith? How did I cultivate a place of joy and rest? What did God teach me in His Word?

**A Look Forward**

As I look forward, what comes to mind?

How do I want to enter tomorrow? How will I cultivate peace in my life?

## The Most Bountiful Kingdom | Psalm 145:13

*Father let me hear from you. Fill my heart, soul, and mind with your presence and discernment from your Holy Spirit. Let your words be a living water quenching my thirst for your goodness.*

# Intro to the Scripture

God's Kingdom is an everlasting Kingdom. No other will bring as much bounty. The reign of God will continue forever and ever. It will never pass away. It will not change as dynasties do among people; it will not be overthrown as they are; its great principles will stand firm forever and ever. It will always have a beautiful bounty. The whole psalm inspires us to affectionately and gratefully praise the Great King of the universe. Amen

**REMEMBER:**

**Read** slowly and prayerfully /Lectio (Read)

**Reflect** /Meditatio (Focus on a word or phrase/listen)

**Respond**/ Oratio (Pray to God)

**Rest**/Contemplate/ Contemplatio (Rest in God)

**Resolve**/Incarnatio (Carry this Word in your life)

Sit quietly for a moment. Take a deep breath in and release. Allow His presence to wash over you.

Begin.

# Lectio Divina Day One

**Psalm 145:13-15 (TPT)** You are the Lord who reigns over your never-ending kingdom through all the ages of time and eternity! You are faithful to fulfill every promise you've made. You manifest yourself as kindness in all you do. Weak and feeble ones you will sustain. Those bent over with burdens of shame you will lift up. You have captured our attention and the eyes of all look to you. You give what they hunger for at just the right time.

**Soul Exploration:**

1.  Do you see yourself as holy and beautiful in God's eyes?

2.  What is Christ's call to you through this scripture?

3.  What wisdom did He give you? How do you see yourself now? Has He removed something?

# Lectio Divina Day Two

**Psalm 145:13-15 (NIV)** Your kingdom is an everlasting kingdom, and your dominion endures through all generations. The LORD is trustworthy in all he promises and faithful in all he does.

**Soul Exploration:**

1. Do you see yourself as holy and beautiful in God's eyes?

2. What is Christ's call to you through this scripture?

3. What wisdom did He give you? How do you see yourself now? Has He removed something?

# Lectio Divina Day Three

**Psalm 145:13-15 (ESV)** "Your kingdom is an everlasting kingdom, and your dominion endures throughout all generations. [The LORD is faithful in all his words and kind in all his works.]"

**Soul Exploration:**

1. Do you see yourself as holy and beautiful in God's eyes?

2. What is Christ's call to you through this scripture?

3. What wisdom did He give you? How do you see yourself now? Has He removed something?

# Lectio Divina Day Four

**Psalm 145:13-15 (KJV)** Thy kingdom is an everlasting kingdom, and thy dominion endureth throughout all generations.

**Soul Exploration:**

1. Do you see yourself as holy and beautiful in God's eyes?

2. What is Christ's call to you through this scripture?

3. What wisdom did He give you? How do you see yourself now? Has He removed something?

# Lectio Divina Day Five

**Psalm 145:13-15 (NASB**) Your kingdom is an everlasting kingdom, and Your dominion endures throughout all generations.

**Soul Exploration:**

1. Do you see yourself as holy and beautiful in God's eyes?

2. What is Christ's call to you through this scripture?

3. What wisdom did He give you? How do you see yourself now? Has He removed something?

# Lectio Divina Day Six

**Psalm 145:13-15 (NLT)** For your kingdom is an everlasting kingdom. You rule throughout all generations. The LORD always keeps his promises; he is gracious in all he does.

**Soul Exploration:**

1.  Do you see yourself as holy and beautiful in God's eyes?

2.  What is Christ's call to you through this scripture?

3.  What wisdom did He give you? How do you see yourself now? Has He removed something?

# Lectio Divina Day Seven

**Psalm 145:13-15 (CSB)** Your kingdom is an everlasting kingdom; your rule is for all generations. The LORD is faithful in all his words and gracious in all his actions.

**Soul Exploration:**

1. Do you see yourself as holy and beautiful in God's eyes?

2. What is Christ's call to you through this scripture?

3. What wisdom did He give you? How do you see yourself now? Has He removed something?

# Weekly Sacred Examen

## A Weekly Reflection

St. Ignatius Loyola's Examen is an opportunity for peaceful reflective prayer. It invites us to find the movement of God in all the people and events of our life. The Examen is simply a set of introspective prompts for you to follow or adapt to your own character and spirit.

Begin with a pause and a slow, deep breath or two; become aware that you are in the presence of a Holy and Beautiful God.

## Thanksgiving

What am I especially grateful for in the past week? (The gift of another day...The love and support I have received...Something I have enjoyed....A moment I felt God's presence.....)

## Petition

I am about to reflect upon my week of Lectio Divina. I ask for the wisdom to know God and to know myself as God sees me.

## Review

What did I learn in the Scriptures I read?

Where did I experience joy?

What troubled me?

What challenged me?

Did I pause and find Selah?

What was something beautiful or holy that was revealed to me?

**Response**

In response to this examen of my life, how have I grown my faith? How did I cultivate a place of joy and rest? What did God teach me in His Word?

**A Look Forward**

As I look forward, what comes to mind?

How do I want to enter tomorrow? How will I cultivate peace in my life?

## Everything Comes from Above | James 1:17

*Father let me hear from you. Fill my heart, soul, and mind with your presence and discernment from your Holy Spirit. Let your words be a living water quenching my thirst for your goodness.*

# Intro to the Scripture

James calls us to make a new list this fall: One of all the good things we do have. Where did all those good things come from? James is encouraging believers in Christ to tell themselves this truth: God gave you every single good thing in your life. He is the source of all the good you have and all the good you crave. Who God is does not change when our circumstances change. He doesn't go from being a good God to a bad God when our trials begin.

He is still the source of all the good in our lives; He never changes. Our seasons in life change like the weather, but God remains the same. Amen

**REMEMBER:**

**Read** slowly and prayerfully /Lectio (Read)

**Reflect** /Meditatio (Focus on a word or phrase/listen)

**Respond**/ Oratio (Pray to God)

**Rest**/Contemplate/ Contemplatio (Rest in God)

**Resolve**/Incarnatio (Carry this Word in your life)

Sit quietly for a moment. Take a deep breath in and release. Allow His presence to wash over you. Begin.

# Lectio Divina Day One

**James 1:16-18 (The Voice)** My dearly loved brothers and sisters, don't be misled. Every good gift bestowed, every perfect gift received comes *to us* from above, courtesy of the Father of lights. He *is consistent.* He won't change His mind or play tricks in the shadows. We have a special role in His plan. He calls us to life by His message of truth so that we will show the rest of His creatures *His goodness and love.*

**Soul Exploration:**

1. Do you see yourself as holy and beautiful in God's eyes?

2. What is Christ's call to you through this scripture?

3. What wisdom did He give you? How do you see yourself now? Has He removed something?

# Lectio Divina Day Two

**James 1:16-18 (NIV)** Every good and perfect gift is from above, coming down from the Father of the heavenly lights, who does not change like shifting shadows.

**Soul Exploration:**

1.  Do you see yourself as holy and beautiful in God's eyes?

2.  What is Christ's call to you through this scripture?

3.  What wisdom did He give you? How do you see yourself now? Has He removed something?

# Lectio Divina Day Three

**James 1:16-18 (ESV)** Every good gift and every perfect gift is from above, coming down from the Father of lights, with whom there is no variation or shadow due to change.

**Soul Exploration:**

1. Do you see yourself as holy and beautiful in God's eyes?

2. What is Christ's call to you through this scripture?

3. What wisdom did He give you? How do you see yourself now? Has He removed something?

# Lectio Divina Day Four

**James 1:16-18 (KJV)** Every good gift and every perfect gift is from above, and cometh down from the Father of lights, with whom is no variableness, neither shadow of turning.

**Soul Exploration:**

1. Do you see yourself as holy and beautiful in God's eyes?

2. What is Christ's call to you through this scripture?

3. What wisdom did He give you? How do you see yourself now? Has He removed something?

# Lectio Divina Day Five

**James 1:16-18 (NASB)** Every good thing given and every perfect gift is from above, coming down from the Father of lights, with whom there is no variation or shifting shadow.

**Soul Exploration:**

1.  Do you see yourself as holy and beautiful in God's eyes?

2.  What is Christ's call to you through this scripture?

3.  What wisdom did He give you? How do you see yourself now? Has He removed something?

# Lectio Divina Day Six

**James 1:16-18 (NLT)** Whatever is good and perfect comes down to us from God our Father, who created all the lights in the heavens. He never changes or casts a shifting shadow.

**Soul Exploration:**

1. Do you see yourself as holy and beautiful in God's eyes?

2. What is Christ's call to you through this scripture?

3. What wisdom did He give you? How do you see yourself now? Has He removed something?

# Lectio Divina Day Seven

**James 1:16-18 (CSB)** Every good and perfect gift is from above, coming down from the Father of lights, who does not change like shifting shadows.

**Soul Exploration:**

1. Do you see yourself as holy and beautiful in God's eyes?

2. What is Christ's call to you through this scripture?

3. What wisdom did He give you? How do you see yourself now? Has He removed something?

# Weekly Sacred Examen

## A Weekly Reflection

St. Ignatius Loyola's Examen is an opportunity for peaceful reflective prayer. It invites us to find the movement of God in all the people and events of our life. The Examen is simply a set of introspective prompts for you to follow or adapt to your own character and spirit.

Begin with a pause and a slow, deep breath or two; become aware that you are in the presence of a Holy and Beautiful God.

## Thanksgiving

What am I especially grateful for in the past week? (The gift of another day...The love and support I have received...Something I have enjoyed….A moment I felt God's presence…..)

## Petition

I am about to reflect upon my week of Lectio Divina. I ask for the wisdom to know God and to know myself as God sees me.

## Review

What did I learn in the Scriptures I read?

Where did I experience joy?

What troubled me?

What challenged me?

Did I pause and find Selah?

What was something beautiful or holy that was revealed to me?

**Response**

In response to this examen of my life, how have I grown my faith? How did I cultivate a place of joy and rest? What did God teach me in His Word?

**A Look Forward**

As I look forward, what comes to mind?

How do I want to enter tomorrow? How will I cultivate peace in my life?

## Be Not Conformed | Romans 12:2

*Father let me hear from you. Fill my heart, soul, and mind with your presence and discernment from your Holy Spirit. Let your words be a living water quenching my thirst for your goodness.*

# Intro to the Scripture

Paul is urging Christians to respond to God's mercy, His forgiveness of our sin, and His inclusion of us in His family. We need to be willing to offer Him our entire lives as a form of living, breathing sacrifice.

Paul also writes that we must no longer be conformed to the world. The word "world" is often used in the New Testament to refer to the "world system," or the way that every human being lives by default. John described this worldly way of living as "the desires of the flesh and the desires of the eyes and pride of life" (1 John 2:16). By instinct, all of us chase those things in pursuit of happiness and meaning. We need to be able to give up the world for Jesus.

**REMEMBER:**

**Read** slowly and prayerfully /Lectio (Read)

**Reflect** /Meditatio (Focus on a word or phrase/listen)

**Respond**/ Oratio (Pray to God)

**Rest**/Contemplate/ Contemplatio (Rest in God)

**Resolve**/Incarnatio (Carry this Word in your life)

Sit quietly for a moment. Take a deep breath in and release. Allow His presence to wash over you.
Begin.

# Lectio Divina Day One

**Romans 12:2 (TPT)** Stop imitating the ideals and opinions of the culture around you but be inwardly transformed by the Holy Spirit through a total reformation of how you think. This will empower you to discern God's will as you live a beautiful life, satisfying and perfect in his eyes.

**Soul Exploration:**

1.  Do you see yourself as holy and beautiful in God's eyes?

2.  What is Christ's call to you through this scripture?

3.  What wisdom did He give you? How do you see yourself now? Has He removed something?

# Lectio Divina Day Two

**Romans 12:2 (NIV)** Do not conform to the pattern of this world but be transformed by the renewing of your mind. Then you will be able to test and approve what God's will is--his good, pleasing and perfect will.

**Soul Exploration:**

1. Do you see yourself as holy and beautiful in God's eyes?

2. What is Christ's call to you through this scripture?

3. What wisdom did He give you? How do you see yourself now? Has He removed something?

# Lectio Divina Day Three

**Romans 12:2 (ESV**) Do not be conformed to this world, but be transformed by the renewal of your mind, that by testing you may discern what is the will of God, what is good and acceptable and perfect.

**Soul Exploration:**

1. Do you see yourself as holy and beautiful in God's eyes?

2. What is Christ's call to you through this scripture?

3. What wisdom did He give you? How do you see yourself now? Has He removed something?

# Lectio Divina Day Four

**Romans 12:2 (KJV)** And be not conformed to this world: but be ye transformed by the renewing of your mind, that ye may prove what *is* that good, and acceptable, and perfect, will of God.

**Soul Exploration:**

1. Do you see yourself as holy and beautiful in God's eyes?

2. What is Christ's call to you through this scripture?

3. What wisdom did He give you? How do you see yourself now? Has He removed something?

# Lectio Divina Day Five

**Romans 12:2 (NASB)** And do not be conformed to this world, but be transformed by the renewing of your mind, so that you may prove what the will of God is, that which is good and acceptable and perfect.

**Soul Exploration:**

1. Do you see yourself as holy and beautiful in God's eyes?

2. What is Christ's call to you through this scripture?

3. What wisdom did He give you? How do you see yourself now? Has He removed something?

# Lectio Divina Day Six

**Romans 12:2 (NLT)** Don't copy the behavior and customs of this world, but let God transform you into a new person by changing the way you think. Then you will learn to know God's will for you, which is good and pleasing and perfect.

**Soul Exploration:**

1. Do you see yourself as holy and beautiful in God's eyes?

2. What is Christ's call to you through this scripture?

3. What wisdom did He give you? How do you see yourself now? Has He removed something?

# Lectio Divina Day Seven

**Romans 12:2 (CSB)** Do not be conformed to this age, but be transformed by the renewing of your mind, so that you may discern what is the good, pleasing, and perfect will of God.

**Soul Exploration:**

1. Do you see yourself as holy and beautiful in God's eyes?

2. What is Christ's call to you through this scripture?

3. What wisdom did He give you? How do you see yourself now? Has He removed something?

# Weekly Sacred Examen

## A Weekly Reflection

St. Ignatius Loyola's Examen is an opportunity for peaceful reflective prayer. It invites us to find the movement of God in all the people and events of our life. The Examen is simply a set of introspective prompts for you to follow or adapt to your own character and spirit.

Begin with a pause and a slow, deep breath or two; become aware that you are in the presence of a Holy and Beautiful God.

## Thanksgiving

What am I especially grateful for in the past week? (The gift of another day...The love and support I have received...Something I have enjoyed....A moment I felt God's presence.....)

## Petition

I am about to reflect upon my week of Lectio Divina. I ask for the wisdom to know God and to know myself as God sees me.

## Review

What did I Learn in the Scriptures I read?

Where did I experience joy?

What troubled me?

What challenged me?

Did I pause and find Selah?

What was something beautiful or holy that was revealed to me?

**Response**

In response to this examen of my life, how have I grown my faith? How did I cultivate a place of joy and rest? What did God teach me in His Word?

**A Look Forward**

As I look forward, what comes to mind?

How do I want to enter tomorrow? How will I cultivate peace in my life?

## Patiently Waiting | James 5:7-8

*Father let me hear from you. Fill my heart, soul, and mind with your presence and discernment from your Holy Spirit. Let your words be a living water quenching my thirst for your goodness.*

# Intro to the Scripture

In this writing from James, we see a promising reminder that just as sure as the seasons come, Jesus' return is assured. His encouragement for us all is patience during suffering. Just as the farmer waits for the rains to quench the thirst of his crops and increase in bountiful harvest, so must we wait patiently for the return of our Savior. Can you imagine the beauty of His return? It will be even more marvelous than the autumn leaves at their peak of grandeur.

**REMEMBER:**

**Read** slowly and prayerfully /Lectio (Read)

**Reflect** /Meditatio (Focus on a word or phrase/listen)

**Respond/** Oratio (Pray to God)

**Rest**/Contemplate/ Contemplatio (Rest in God)

**Resolve**/Incarnatio (Carry this Word in your life)

Sit quietly for a moment. Take a deep breath in and release. Allow His presence to wash over you.
Begin.

# Lectio Divina Day One

**James 5: 7-8 (NIV)** Be patient, then, brothers and sisters, until the Lord's coming. See how the farmer waits for the land to yield its valuable crop, patiently waiting for the autumn and spring rains. You too, be patient and stand firm, because the Lord's coming is near.

**Soul Exploration:**

1.   Do you see yourself as holy and beautiful in God's eyes?

2.   What is Christ's call to you through this scripture?

3.   What wisdom did He give you? How do you see yourself now? Has He removed something?

# Lectio Divina Day Two

**James 5: 7-8 (TPL)** Meanwhile, brothers and sisters, we must be patient and filled with expectation as we wait for the appearing of the Lord. Think about the farmer who has to patiently wait for the earth's harvest as it ripens because of the early and latter rains.  So you also keep your hopes high and be patient, for the presence of the Lord is drawing closer.

**Soul Exploration:**

1.  Do you see yourself as holy and beautiful in God's eyes?

2.  What is Christ's call to you through this scripture?

3.  What wisdom did He give you? How do you see yourself now? Has He removed something?

# Lectio Divina Day Three

**James 5: 7-8 (ESV)** Be patient, therefore, brothers, until the coming of the Lord. See how the farmer waits for the precious fruit of the earth, being patient about it, until it receives the early and the late rains. You also, be patient. Establish your hearts, for the coming of the Lord is at hand.

**Soul Exploration:**

1. Do you see yourself as holy and beautiful in God's eyes?

2. What is Christ's call to you through this scripture?

3. What wisdom did He give you? How do you see yourself now? Has He removed something?

# Lectio Divina Day Four

**James 5: 7-8 (KJV)** Be patient therefore, brethren, unto the coming of the Lord. Behold, the husbandman waiteth for the precious fruit of the earth, and hath long patience for it, until he receives the early and latter rain. Be ye also patient; establish your hearts: for the coming of the Lord draweth nigh.

**Soul Exploration:**

1. Do you see yourself as holy and beautiful in God's eyes?

2. What is Christ's call to you through this scripture?

3. What wisdom did He give you? How do you see yourself now? Has He removed something?

# Lectio Divina Day Five

**James 5: 7-8 (NASB)** Therefore be patient, brethren, until the coming of the Lord. The farmer waits for the precious produce of the soil, being patient about it, until it gets the early and late rains. You too be patient; strengthen your hearts, for the coming of the Lord is near.

**Soul Exploration:**

1. Do you see yourself as holy and beautiful in God's eyes?

2. What is Christ's call to you through this scripture?

3. What wisdom did He give you? How do you see yourself now? Has He removed something?

# Lectio Divina Day Six

**James 5: 7-8 (NRSVCE)** Be patient, therefore, beloved, until the coming of the Lord. The farmer waits for the precious crop from the earth, being patient with it until it receives the early and the late rains. You also must be patient. Strengthen your hearts, for the coming of the Lord is near.

**Soul Exploration:**

1. Do you see yourself as holy and beautiful in God's eyes?

2. What is Christ's call to you through this scripture?

3. What wisdom did He give you? How do you see yourself now? Has He removed something?

# Lectio Divina Day Seven

**James 5: 7-8 (CSB)** Therefore, brothers and sisters, be patient until the Lord's coming. See how the farmer waits for the precious fruit of the earth and is patient with it until it receives the early and the late rains. You also must be patient. Strengthen your hearts, because the Lord's coming is near.

**Soul Exploration:**

1. Do you see yourself as holy and beautiful in God's eyes?

2. What is Christ's call to you through this scripture?

3. What wisdom did He give you? How do you see yourself now? Has He removed something?

# Weekly Sacred Examen

## A Weekly Reflection

St. Ignatius Loyola's Examen is an opportunity for peaceful reflective prayer. It invites us to find the movement of God in all the people and events of our life. The Examen is simply a set of introspective prompts for you to follow or adapt to your own character and spirit.

Begin with a pause and a slow, deep breath or two; become aware that you are in the presence of a Holy and Beautiful God.

## Thanksgiving

What am I especially grateful for in the past week? (The gift of another day...The love and support I have received...Something I have enjoyed....A moment I felt God's presence.....)

## Petition

I am about to reflect upon my week of Lectio Divina. I ask for the wisdom to know God and to know myself as God sees me.

## Review

What did I learn in the Scriptures I read?

Where did I experience joy?

What troubled me?

What challenged me?

Did I pause and find Selah?

What was something beautiful or holy that was revealed to me?

## Response

In response to this examen of my life, how have I grown my faith? How did I cultivate a place of joy and rest? What did God teach me in His Word?

## A Look Forward

As I look forward, what comes to mind?

How do I want to enter tomorrow? How will I cultivate peace in my life?

## A New Life in Christ | Colossians 2:6-7

*Father let me hear from you. Fill my heart, soul, and mind with your presence and discernment from your Holy Spirit. Let your words be a living water quenching my thirst for your goodness.*

# Intro to the Scripture

In this verse, Paul makes a beautiful statement about our walk with Christ. The Colossians, like all other saved believers, received Christ by faith. Paul's implication is that those who accepted Christ in faith ought to "walk"—to live and think—by faith, as well. The false teachings confronting Colossae emphasized works and personal sacrifice as the means to pleasing God. It is true that works are a vital aspect of our faith walk (1 John 3:17–18), but these are the *results* of saving faith, not the source of it. Our walk with God must be rooted in faith—and therefore rooted in Him, not us—just as salvation is. This is the path to a faith that is truly holy and beautiful.

**REMEMBER:**

**Read** slowly and prayerfully /Lectio (Read)

**Reflect** /Meditatio (Focus on a word or phrase/listen)

**Respond/** Oratio (Pray to God)

**Rest/**Contemplate/ Contemplatio (Rest in God)

**Resolve/**Incarnatio (Carry this Word in your life)

Sit quietly for a moment. Take a deep breath in and release. Allow His presence to wash over you.
Begin.

# Lectio Divina Day One

**Colossians 2:6-7 (TPT)** In the same way you received Jesus our Lord and Messiah by faith, continue your journey of faith, progressing further into your union with him! [7] Your spiritual roots go deeply into his life as you are continually infused with strength, encouraged in every way. For you are established in the faith you have absorbed and enriched by your devotion to him!

**Soul Exploration:**

1. Do you see yourself as holy and beautiful in God's eyes?

2. What is Christ's call to you through this scripture?

3. What wisdom did He give you? How do you see yourself now? Has He removed something?

# Lectio Divina Day Two

**Colossians 2:6-7 (NIV)** So then, just as you received Christ Jesus as Lord, continue to live your lives in him.

### Soul Exploration:

1. Do you see yourself as holy and beautiful in God's eyes?

2. What is Christ's call to you through this scripture?

3. What wisdom did He give you? How do you see yourself now? Has He removed something?

# Lectio Divina Day Three

**Colossians 2:6-7 (ESV)** Therefore, as you received Christ Jesus the Lord, so walk in him.

**Soul Exploration:**

1.  Do you see yourself as holy and beautiful in God's eyes?

2.  What is Christ's call to you through this scripture?

3.  What wisdom did He give you? How do you see yourself now? Has He removed something?

# Lectio Divina Day Four

**Colossians 2:6-7 (KJV)** As ye have therefore received Christ Jesus the Lord, *so* walk ye in him.

### Soul Exploration:

1. Do you see yourself as holy and beautiful in God's eyes?

2. What is Christ's call to you through this scripture?

3. What wisdom did He give you? How do you see yourself now? Has He removed something?

# Lectio Divina Day Five

**Colossians 2:6-7 (NASB)** Therefore as you have received Christ Jesus the Lord, so walk in Him.

**Soul Exploration:**

1.  Do you see yourself as holy and beautiful in God's eyes?

2.  What is Christ's call to you through this scripture?

3.  What wisdom did He give you? How do you see yourself now? Has He removed something?

# Lectio Divina Day Six

**Colossians 2:6-7 (NLT)** And now, just as you accepted Christ Jesus as your Lord, you must continue to follow him.

**Soul Exploration:**

1. Do you see yourself as holy and beautiful in God's eyes?

2. What is Christ's call to you through this scripture?

3. What wisdom did He give you? How do you see yourself now? Has He removed something?

# Lectio Divina Day Seven

**Colossians 2:6-7 (CSB)** So then, just as you have received Christ Jesus as Lord, continue to live in him.

**Soul Exploration:**

1. Do you see yourself as holy and beautiful in God's eyes?

2. What is Christ's call to you through this scripture?

3. What wisdom did He give you? How do you see yourself now? Has He removed something?

# Weekly Sacred Examen

## A Weekly Reflection

St. Ignatius Loyola's Examen is an opportunity for peaceful reflective prayer. It invites us to find the movement of God in all the people and events of our life. The Examen is simply a set of introspective prompts for you to follow or adapt to your own character and spirit.

Begin with a pause and a slow, deep breath or two; become aware that you are in the presence of a Holy and Beautiful God.

## Thanksgiving

What am I especially grateful for in the past week? (The gift of another day...The love and support I have received...Something I have enjoyed….A moment I felt God's presence…..)

## Petition

I am about to reflect upon my week of Lectio Divina. I ask for the wisdom to know God and to know myself as God sees me.

## Review

What did I learn in the Scriptures I read?

Where did I experience joy?

What troubled me?

What challenged me?

Did I pause and find Selah?

What was something beautiful or holy that was revealed to me?

## Response

In response to this examen of my life, how have I grown my faith? How did I cultivate a place of joy and rest? What did God teach me in His Word?

## A Look Forward

As I look forward, what comes to mind?

How do I want to enter tomorrow? How will I cultivate peace in my life?

*Father let me hear from you. Fill my heart, soul, and mind with your presence and discernment from your Holy Spirit. Let your words be a living water quenching my thirst for your goodness.*

## Intro to the Scripture

As Christians we have an amazing source of confident hope and encouragement – The Holy and Beautiful Jesus Christ/ King of Kings.

For us to become spiritually mature, we need to experience a sense of confidence in our faith. That assurance should come naturally when we consider examples such as Abraham. He was given promises by God, and history proved those promises to be true.

**REMEMBER:**

**Read** slowly and prayerfully /Lectio (Read)

**Reflect** /Meditatio (Focus on a word or phrase/listen)

**Respond/** Oratio (Pray to God)

**Rest**/Contemplate/ Contemplatio (Rest in God)

**Resolve**/Incarnatio (Carry this Word in your life)

Sit quietly for a moment. Take a deep breath in and release. Allow His presence to wash over you.
Begin.

# Lectio Divina Day One

**Hebrews 6:19 (Voice)** So God has given us two unchanging things: *His promise and His oath.* These prove that it is impossible for God to lie. As a result, we who come to God for refuge might be encouraged to seize that hope that is set before us. **That hope is real and true, an anchor to steady our *restless* souls, a hope that leads us back behind the curtain *to where God is*** *(as the high priests did in the days when reconciliation flowed from sacrifices in the temple)* and back into the place where Jesus, who went ahead on our behalf, has entered since He has become a High Priest forever in the order of Melchizedek.

**Soul Exploration:**

1. Do you see yourself as holy and beautiful in God's eyes?

2. What is Christ's call to you through this scripture?

3. What wisdom did He give you? How do you see yourself now? Has He removed something?

# Lectio Divina Day Two

**Hebrews 6:19 (TPT)** We have this certain hope like a strong, unbreakable anchor holding our souls to God himself. Our anchor of hope is fastened *to the mercy seat* which sits in the heavenly realm beyond the sacred threshold

**Soul Exploration:**

1.  Do you see yourself as holy and beautiful in God's eyes?

2.  What is Christ's call to you through this scripture?

3.  What wisdom did He give you? How do you see yourself now? Has He removed something?

# Lectio Divina Day Three

**Hebrews 6:19 (NIV)** We have this hope as an anchor for the soul, firm and secure. It enters the inner sanctuary behind the curtain.

**Soul Exploration:**

1. Do you see yourself as holy and beautiful in God's eyes?

2. What is Christ's call to you through this scripture?

3. What wisdom did He give you? How do you see yourself now? Has He removed something?

# Lectio Divina Day Four

**Hebrews 6:19 (ESV)** We have this as a sure and steadfast anchor of the soul, a hope that enters into the inner place behind the curtain.

**Soul Exploration:**

1.  Do you see yourself as holy and beautiful in God's eyes?

2.  What is Christ's call to you through this scripture?

3.  What wisdom did He give you? How do you see yourself now? Has He removed something?

# Lectio Divina Day Five

**Hebrews 6:19 (KJV)** Which *hope* we have as an anchor of the soul, both sure and steadfast, and which entereth into that within the veil.

**Soul Exploration:**

1. Do you see yourself as holy and beautiful in God's eyes?

2. What is Christ's call to you through this scripture?

3. What wisdom did He give you? How do you see yourself now? Has He removed something?

# Lectio Divina Day Six

**Hebrews 6:19 (NASB)** This hope we have as an anchor of the soul, a hope both sure and steadfast and one which enters within the veil.

**Soul Exploration:**

1. Do you see yourself as holy and beautiful in God's eyes?

2. What is Christ's call to you through this scripture?

3. What wisdom did He give you? How do you see yourself now? Has He removed something?

# Lectio Divina Day Seven

**Hebrews 6:19 (NLT)** This hope is a strong and trustworthy anchor for our souls. It leads us through the curtain into God's inner sanctuary.

**Soul Exploration:**

1. Do you see yourself as holy and beautiful in God's eyes?

2. What is Christ's call to you through this scripture?

3. What wisdom did He give you? How do you see yourself now? Has He removed something?

# Weekly Sacred Examen

## A Weekly Reflection

St. Ignatius Loyola's Examen is an opportunity for peaceful reflective prayer. It invites us to find the movement of God in all the people and events of our life. The Examen is simply a set of introspective prompts for you to follow or adapt to your own character and spirit.

Begin with a pause and a slow, deep breath or two; become aware that you are in the presence of a Holy and Beautiful God.

## Thanksgiving

What am I especially grateful for in the past week? (The gift of another day...The love and support I have received...Something I have enjoyed.... A moment I felt God's presence....)

## Petition

I am about to reflect upon my week of Lectio Divina. I ask for the wisdom to know God and to know myself as God sees me.

## Review

What did I learn in the Scriptures I read?

Where did I experience joy?

What troubled me?

What challenged me?

Did I pause and find Selah?

What was something beautiful or holy that was revealed to me?

## Response

In response to this examen of my life, how have I grown my faith? How did I cultivate a place of joy and rest? What did God teach me in His Word?

## A Look Forward

As I look forward, what comes to mind?

How do I want to enter tomorrow? How will I cultivate peace in my life?

*Father let me hear from you. Fill my heart, soul, and mind with your presence and discernment from your Holy Spirit. Let your words be a living water quenching my thirst for your goodness.*

## Intro to the Scripture

Psalm 106 is a history of the goodness of God to Israel. It is also a history of their rebellions and sins, yet it begins and ends with Hallelujah. Even in their sinful state, they praised God and confessed. Their badness made His goodness more apparent. We must confess our own sin and praise His for His goodness.  Our sin must never keep us from praising and drawing closer to God.

**REMEMBER:**

**Read** slowly and prayerfully /Lectio (Read)

**Reflect** /Meditatio (Focus on a word or phrase/listen)

**Respond/** Oratio (Pray to God)

**Rest**/Contemplate/ Contemplatio (Rest in God)

**Resolve**/Incarnatio (Carry this Word in your life)

Sit quietly for a moment. Take a deep breath in and release. Allow His presence to wash over you.
Begin.

# Lectio Divina Day One

**Psalm 106:1 (TPT)** Hallelujah! Praise the Lord! Everyone thank God, for he is good and easy to please.
Your tender love for us, Lord, continues on forever.

**Soul Exploration:**

1.  Do you see yourself as holy and beautiful in God's eyes?

2.  What is Christ's call to you through this scripture?

3.  What wisdom did He give you? How do you see yourself now? Has He removed something?

# Lectio Divina Day Two

**Psalm 106:1 (NIV)** Praise the Lord. Give thanks to the Lord, for he is good; his love endures forever.

**Soul Exploration:**

1.  Do you see yourself as holy and beautiful in God's eyes?

2.  What is Christ's call to you through this scripture?

3.  What wisdom did He give you? How do you see yourself now? Has He removed something?

# Lectio Divina Day Three

**Psalm 106:1 (ESV)** Praise the Lord! Oh, give thanks to the Lord, for he is good, for his steadfast love endures forever!

**Soul Exploration:**

1. Do you see yourself as holy and beautiful in God's eyes?

2. What is Christ's call to you through this scripture?

3. What wisdom did He give you? How do you see yourself now? Has He removed something?

# Lectio Divina Day Four

**Psalm 106:1 (KJV)** Praise ye the Lord. O give thanks unto the Lord; for he is good: for his mercy endureth forever.

**Soul Exploration:**

1. Do you see yourself as holy and beautiful in God's eyes?

2. What is Christ's call to you through this scripture?

3. What wisdom did He give you? How do you see yourself now? Has He removed something?

# Lectio Divina Day Five

**Psalm 106:1 (NASB)** Praise the LORD! Oh, give thanks to the LORD, for He is good; For His lovingkindness is everlasting.

**Soul Exploration:**

1. Do you see yourself as holy and beautiful in God's eyes?

2. What is Christ's call to you through this scripture?

3. What wisdom did He give you? How do you see yourself now? Has He removed something?

# Lectio Divina Day Six

**Psalm 106:1 (NRSVCE)** Praise the LORD! O give thanks to the LORD, for he is good; for his steadfast love endures forever.

**Soul Exploration:**

1. Do you see yourself as holy and beautiful in God's eyes?

2. What is Christ's call to you through this scripture?

3. What wisdom did He give you? How do you see yourself now? Has He removed something?

# Lectio Divina Day Seven

**Psalm 106:1 (CSB)** Hallelujah! Give thanks to the LORD, for he is good; his faithful love endures forever.

**Soul Exploration:**

1. Do you see yourself as holy and beautiful in God's eyes?

2. What is Christ's call to you through this scripture?

3. What wisdom did He give you? How do you see yourself now? Has He removed something?

# Weekly Sacred Examen

## A Weekly Reflection

St. Ignatius Loyola's Examen is an opportunity for peaceful reflective prayer. It invites us to find the movement of God in all the people and events of our life. The Examen is simply a set of introspective prompts for you to follow or adapt to your own character and spirit.

Begin with a pause and a slow, deep breath or two; become aware that you are in the presence of a Holy and Beautiful God.

## Thanksgiving

What am I especially grateful for in the past week? (The gift of another day...The love and support I have received...Something I have enjoyed....A moment I felt God's presence.....)

## Petition

I am about to reflect upon my week of Lectio Divina. I ask for the wisdom to know God and to know myself as God sees me.

**Review**

What did I learn in the Scriptures I read?

Where did I experience joy?

What troubled me?

What challenged me?

Did I pause and find Selah?

What was something beautiful or holy that was revealed to me?

## Response

In response to this examen of my life, how have I grown my faith? How did I cultivate a place of joy and rest? What did God teach me in His Word?

## A Look Forward

As I look forward, what comes to mind?

How do I want to enter tomorrow? How will I cultivate peace in my life?

## Impossible Made Possible | 1 Thessalonians 5:16-18

*Father let me hear from you. Fill my heart, soul, and mind with your presence and discernment from your Holy Spirit. Let your words be a living water quenching my thirst for your goodness.*

# Intro to the Scripture

Paul offered no explanation on these commands. He mentions them and moves on, yet the importance of these words is great. They are a reminder of our need for the Holy Spirit in our daily lives so that we may continuously feast on God's joy and be thankful in prayer all throughout our lives. In our flesh, we often find ourselves unable to follow the commands God gives us throughout the Bible. These three are the most difficult, if not impossible, commands to achieve, yet when we rely on the indwelling of the Holy Spirit, we find our ability increased.

**REMEMBER:**

**Read** slowly and prayerfully /Lectio (Read)

**Reflect** /Meditatio (Focus on a word or phrase/listen)

**Respond/** Oratio (Pray to God)

**Rest/**Contemplate/ Contemplatio (Rest in God)

**Resolve/**Incarnatio (Carry this Word in your life)


Sit quietly for a moment. Take a deep breath in and release. Allow His presence to wash over you.
Begin.

# Lectio Divina Day One

**1 Thessalonians 5:16-18 (TPT)** Let joy be your continual feast. Make your life a prayer. And in the midst of everything be always giving thanks, for this is God's perfect plan for you in Christ Jesus.

**Soul Exploration:**

1.  Do you see yourself as holy and beautiful in God's eyes?

2.  What is Christ's call to you through this scripture?

3.  What wisdom did He give you? How do you see yourself now? Has He removed something?

# Lectio Divina Day Two

**1 Thessalonians 5:16-18 (NIV)** Rejoice always, pray continually, give thanks in all circumstances; for this is God's will for you in Christ Jesus.

**Soul Exploration:**

1. Do you see yourself as holy and beautiful in God's eyes?

2. What is Christ's call to you through this scripture?

3. What wisdom did He give you? How do you see yourself now? Has He removed something?

# Lectio Divina Day Three

**1 Thessalonians 5:16-18 (ESV)** Rejoice always, pray without ceasing, give thanks in all circumstances; for this is the will of God in Christ Jesus for you.

**Soul Exploration:**

1. Do you see yourself as holy and beautiful in God's eyes?

2. What is Christ's call to you through this scripture?

3. What wisdom did He give you? How do you see yourself now? Has He removed something?

# Lectio Divina Day Four

**1 Thessalonians 5:16-18 (KJV)** Rejoice evermore. Pray without ceasing. In everything give thanks: for this is the will of God in Christ Jesus concerning you.

**Soul Exploration:**

1. Do you see yourself as holy and beautiful in God's eyes?

2. What is Christ's call to you through this scripture?

3. What wisdom did He give you? How do you see yourself now? Has He removed something?

# Lectio Divina Day Five

**1 Thessalonians 5:16-18 (NASB)** Rejoice always; pray without ceasing; in everything give thanks; for this is God's will for you in Christ Jesus.

**Soul Exploration:**

1. Do you see yourself as holy and beautiful in God's eyes?

2. What is Christ's call to you through this scripture?

3. What wisdom did He give you? How do you see yourself now? Has He removed something?

# Lectio Divina Day Six

**1 Thessalonians 5:16-18 (NRSVCE)** Rejoice always, pray without ceasing, give thanks in all circumstances; for this is the will of God in Christ Jesus for you.

**Soul Exploration:**

1.  Do you see yourself as holy and beautiful in God's eyes?

2.  What is Christ's call to you through this scripture?

3.  What wisdom did He give you? How do you see yourself now? Has He removed something?

# Lectio Divina Day Seven

**1 Thessalonians 5:16-18 (CSB)** Rejoice always, pray constantly, give thanks in everything; for this is God's will for you in Christ Jesus.

**Soul Exploration:**

1. Do you see yourself as holy and beautiful in God's eyes?

2. What is Christ's call to you through this scripture?

3. What wisdom did He give you? How do you see yourself now? Has He removed something?

# Weekly Sacred Examen

## A Weekly Reflection

St. Ignatius Loyola's Examen is an opportunity for peaceful reflective prayer. It invites us to find the movement of God in all the people and events of our life. The Examen is simply a set of introspective prompts for you to follow or adapt to your own character and spirit.

Begin with a pause and a slow, deep breath or two; become aware that you are in the presence of a Holy and Beautiful God.

## Thanksgiving

What am I especially grateful for in the past week? (The gift of another day...The love and support I have received...Something I have enjoyed….A moment I felt God's presence…..)

## Petition

I am about to reflect upon my week of Lectio Divina. I ask for the wisdom to know God and to know myself as God sees me.

## Review

What did I learn in the Scriptures I read?

Where did I experience joy?

What troubled me?

What challenged me?

Did I pause and find Selah?

What was something beautiful or holy that was revealed to me?

**Response**

In response to this examen of my life, how have I grown my faith? How did I cultivate a place of joy and rest? What did God teach me in His Word?

**A Look Forward**

As I look forward, what comes to mind?

How do I want to enter tomorrow? How will I cultivate peace in my life?

## Hope | Matthew 1:18-24

*Father let me hear from you. Fill my heart, soul, and mind with your presence and discernment from your Holy Spirit. Let your words be a living water quenching my thirst for your goodness.*

# Intro to the Scripture

Joseph, the son of David, takes the pregnant Mary as his wife in obedience to God after an angel visits him in a dream. In this passage, God is doing a new and an old thing. This event is an intentional action of "God with us." Joseph accepts Jesus as His son. God's anointed One, was born.

**REMEMBER:**

**Read** slowly and prayerfully /Lectio (Read)

**Reflect** /Meditatio (Focus on a word or phrase/listen)

**Respond/** Oratio (Pray to God)

**Rest/**Contemplate/ Contemplatio (Rest in God)

**Resolve/**Incarnatio (Carry this Word in your life)

Sit quietly for a moment. Take a deep breath in and release. Allow His presence to wash over you.
Begin.

# Lectio Divina Day One

**Matthew 1:18-24 (TPT)** This was how Jesus, God's Anointed One, was born. His mother, Mary, had promised Joseph to be his wife, but *while she was still a virgin,* she became pregnant through the power of the Holy Spirit. Her fiancé, Joseph, was a righteous man full of integrity and he didn't want to disgrace her, but when he learned of her pregnancy, he secretly planned to break the engagement. While he was still debating with himself about what to do, he fell asleep and had a supernatural dream. An angel from the Lord appeared to him in clear light and said, "Joseph, descendant of David, don't hesitate to takc Mary into your home as your wife, because the power of the Holy Spirit has conceived a child in her womb. She will give birth to a son, and you are to name him 'Savior,' for he is destined to give his life to save his people from their sins." This happened so that what the Lord spoke through his prophet would come true:

Listen! A virgin will be pregnant, she will give birth to a Son, and he will be known as "Emmanuel," which means in Hebrew, "God became one of us."

When Joseph awoke from his dream, he did all that the angel of the Lord instructed him to do. He took Mary to be his wife.

**Soul Exploration:**

1. Do you see yourself as holy and beautiful in God's eyes?

2. What is Christ's call to you through this scripture?

3. What wisdom did He give you? How do you see yourself now? Has He removed something?

# Lectio Divina Day Two

**Matthew 1:18-24 (NIV)** This is how the birth of Jesus the Messiah came about: His mother Mary was pledged to be married to Joseph, but before they came together, she was found to be pregnant through the Holy Spirit. Because Joseph her husband was faithful to the law, and yet did not want to expose her to public disgrace, he had in mind to divorce her quietly.

But after he had considered this, an angel of the Lord appeared to him in a dream and said, "Joseph son of David, do not be afraid to take Mary home as your wife, because what is conceived in her is from the Holy Spirit. She will give birth to a son, and you are to give him the name Jesus, because he will save his people from their sins."

All this took place to fulfill what the Lord had said through the prophet: "The virgin will conceive and give birth to a son, and they will call him Immanuel" (which means "God with us").

When Joseph woke up, he did what the angel of the Lord had commanded him and took Mary home as his wife.

**Soul Exploration:**

1. Do you see yourself as holy and beautiful in God's eyes?

2. What is Christ's call to you through this scripture?

3. What wisdom did He give you? How do you see yourself now? Has He removed something?

# Lectio Divina Day Three

**Matthew 1:18-24 (NASB)** Now the birth of Jesus Christ was as follows: when His mother Mary had been betrothed to Joseph, before they came together, she was found to be with child by the Holy Spirit. And Joseph her husband, being a righteous man and not wanting to disgrace her, planned to send her away secretly. But when he had considered this, behold, an angel of the Lord appeared to him in a dream, saying, "Joseph, son of David, do not be afraid to take Mary as your wife; for the Child who has been conceived in her is of the Holy Spirit. She will bear a Son; and you shall call His name Jesus, for He will save His people from their sins." Now all this took place to fulfill what was spoken by the Lord through the prophet: "BEHOLD, THE VIRGIN SHALL BE WITH CHILD AND SHALL BEAR A SON, AND THEY SHALL CALL HIS NAME IMMANUEL," which translated means, "GOD WITH US." And Joseph awoke from his sleep and did as the angel of the Lord commanded him and took *Mary* as his wife.

### Soul Exploration:

1. Do you see yourself as holy and beautiful in God's eyes?

2. What is Christ's call to you through this scripture?

3. What wisdom did He give you? How do you see yourself now? Has He removed something?

# Lectio Divina Day Four

**Matthew 1:18-24 (MSG)** The birth of Jesus took place like this. His mother, Mary, was engaged to be married to Joseph. Before they came to the marriage bed, Joseph discovered she was pregnant. (It was by the Holy Spirit, but he didn't know that.) Joseph, chagrined but noble, determined to take care of things quietly so Mary would not be disgraced.

While he was trying to figure a way out, he had a dream. God's angel spoke in the dream: "Joseph, son of David, don't hesitate to get married. Mary's pregnancy is Spirit-conceived. God's Holy Spirit has made her pregnant. She will bring a son to birth, and when she does, you, Joseph, will name him Jesus—'God saves'—because he will save his people from their sins." This would bring the prophet's embryonic sermon to full term:

Watch for this—a virgin will get pregnant and bear a son; They will name him Immanuel (Hebrew for "God is with us"). Then Joseph woke up. He did exactly what God's angel commanded in the dream: He married Mary. But he did not consummate the marriage until she had the baby. He named the baby Jesus.

**Soul Exploration:**

1. Do you see yourself as holy and beautiful in God's eyes?

2. What is Christ's call to you through this scripture?

3. What wisdom did He give you? How do you see yourself now? Has He removed something?

# Lectio Divina Day Five

**Matthew 1:18-24 (KJV)** Now the birth of Jesus Christ was on this wise: When as his mother Mary was espoused to Joseph, before they came together, she was found with child of the Holy Ghost.
Then Joseph her husband, being a just man, and not willing to make her a public example, was minded to put her away privily.

But while he thought on these things, behold, the angel of the LORD appeared unto him in a dream, saying, Joseph, thou son of David, fear not to take unto thee Mary thy wife: for that which is conceived in her is of the Holy Ghost.

And she shall bring forth a son, and thou shalt call his name JESUS: for he shall save his people from their sins.

Now all this was done, that it might be fulfilled which was spoken of the Lord by the prophet, saying,
Behold, a virgin shall be with child, and shall bring forth a son, and they shall call his name Emmanuel, which being interpreted is, God with us.
Then Joseph being raised from sleep did as the angel of the Lord had bidden him and took unto him his wife.

**Soul Exploration:**

1.  Do you see yourself as holy and beautiful in God's eyes?

2.  What is Christ's call to you through this scripture?

3.  What wisdom did He give you? How do you see yourself now? Has He removed something?

# Lectio Divina Day Six

**Matthew 1:18-24 (ESV) Now** the birth of Jesus Christ took place in this way. When his mother Mary had been betrothed to Joseph, before they came together, she was found to be with child from the Holy Spirit. And her husband Joseph, being a just man and unwilling to put her to shame, resolved to divorce her quietly. But as he considered these things, behold, an angel of the Lord appeared to him in a dream, saying, "Joseph, son of David, do not fear to take Mary as your wife, for that which is conceived in her is from the Holy Spirit. She will bear a son, and you shall call his name Jesus, for he will save his people from their sins." All this took place to fulfill what the Lord had spoken by the prophet: "Behold, the virgin shall conceive and bear a son, and they shall call his name Immanuel" (which means, God with us). When Joseph woke from sleep, he did as the angel of the Lord commanded him: he took his wife.

**Soul Exploration:**

1. Do you see yourself as holy and beautiful in God's eyes?

2. What is Christ's call to you through this scripture?

3. What wisdom did He give you? How do you see yourself now? Has He removed something?

# Lectio Divina Day Seven

**Matthew 1:18-24 (NET)** Now the birth of Jesus Christ happened this way. While his mother Mary was engaged to Joseph, but before they came together, she was found to be pregnant through the Holy Spirit. Because Joseph, her husband to be, was a righteous man, and because he did not want to disgrace her, he intended to divorce her privately. When he had contemplated this, an angel of the Lord appeared to him in a dream and said, "Joseph, son of David, do not be afraid to take Mary as your wife, because the child conceived in her is from the Holy Spirit. She will give birth to a son, and you will name him Jesus, because he will save his people from their sins." This all happened so that what was spoken by the Lord through the prophet would be fulfilled: "***Look! The virgin will conceive and give birth to a son, and*** *they* ***will name him Emmanuel***," which means "***God with us***." When Joseph awoke from sleep, he did what the angel of the Lord told him. He took his wife.

**Soul Exploration:**

1. Do you see yourself as holy and beautiful in God's eyes?

2. What is Christ's call to you through this scripture?

3. What wisdom did He give you? How do you see yourself now? Has He removed something?

# Weekly Sacred Examen

## A Weekly Reflection

St. Ignatius Loyola's Examen is an opportunity for peaceful reflective prayer. It invites us to find the movement of God in all the people and events of our life. The Examen is simply a set of introspective prompts for you to follow or adapt to your own character and spirit.

Begin with a pause and a slow, deep breath or two; become aware that you are in the presence of a Holy and Beautiful God.

## Thanksgiving

What am I especially grateful for in the past week? (The gift of another day...The love and support I have received...Something I have enjoyed….A moment I felt God's presence…..)

## Petition

I am about to reflect upon my week of Lectio Divina. I ask for the wisdom to know God and to know myself as God sees me.

## Review

What did I learn in the Scriptures I read?

Where did I experience joy?

What troubled me?

What challenged me?

Did I pause and find Selah?

What was something beautiful or holy that was revealed to me?

## Response

In response to this examen of my life, how have I grown my faith? How did I cultivate a place of joy and rest? What did God teach me in His Word?

## A Look Forward

As I look forward, what comes to mind?

How do I want to enter tomorrow? How will I cultivate peace in my life?

# Peace | Luke 1:26-38

*Father let me hear from you. Fill my heart, soul, and mind with your presence and discernment from your Holy Spirit. Let your words be a living water quenching my thirst for your goodness.*

## Intro to the Scripture:

Just like her husband, Mary, too, was approached by an angel. She questioned how she could have a baby since she had never had sexual relations. The Holy Spirit, the presence of God, was to overshadow Mary. Mary had a servant's heart and was completely submissive to God. She showed a holy and beautiful confidence in the Lord. Mary models an attitude of obedience and trust for us to follow.

**REMEMBER:**

**Read** slowly and prayerfully /Lectio (Read)

**Reflect** /Meditatio (Focus on a word or phrase/listen)

**Respond/** Oratio (Pray to God)

**Rest**/Contemplate/ Contemplatio (Rest in God)

**Resolve**/Incarnatio (Carry this Word in your life)

Sit quietly for a moment. Take a deep breath in and release. Allow His presence to wash over you.
Begin.

# Lectio Divina Day One

**Luke 1:26-38 (TPT)** During the sixth month of Elizabeth's pregnancy, the angel Gabriel was sent from God's presence to an unmarried girl named Mary, living in Nazareth, a village in Galilee. She was engaged to a man named Joseph, a true descendant of King David. Gabriel appeared to her and said, "Grace to you, young woman, for the Lord is with you and so you are anointed with great favor."

Mary was deeply troubled over the words of the angel and bewildered over what this may mean for her. But the angel reassured her, saying, "Do not yield to your fear, Mary, for the Lord has found delight in you and has chosen to surprise you with a wonderful gift. You will become pregnant with a baby boy, and you are to name him Jesus. He will be supreme and will be known as the Son of the Highest. And the Lord God will enthrone him as King on his ancestor David's throne. He will reign as King of Israel forever, and his reign will have no limit."

Mary said, "But how could this happen? I am still a virgin!"

Gabriel answered, "The Spirit of Holiness will fall upon you and almighty God will spread his shadow of power over you in a cloud of glory! This is why the child born to you will be holy, and he will be called the Son of God. What's more, your aged aunt, Elizabeth, has also become pregnant with a son. The 'barren one' is now in her sixth month. Not one promise from God is empty of power, for nothing is impossible with God!"

Then Mary responded, saying, "This is amazing! I will be a mother for the Lord! As his servant, I accept whatever he has for me. May everything you have told me come to pass." And the angel left her.

**Soul Exploration:**

1. Do you see yourself as holy and beautiful in God's eyes?

2. What is Christ's call to you through this scripture?

3. What wisdom did He give you? How do you see yourself now? Has He removed something?

# Lectio Divina Day Two

**Luke 1:26-38 (NIV)** In the sixth month of Elizabeth's pregnancy, God sent the angel Gabriel to Nazareth, a town in Galilee, to a virgin pledged to be married to a man named Joseph, a descendant of David. The virgin's name was Mary. The angel went to her and said, "Greetings, you who are highly favored! The Lord is with you."
Mary was greatly troubled at his words and wondered what kind of greeting this might be. But the angel said to her, "Do not be afraid, Mary; you have found favor with God. You will conceive and give birth to a son, and you are to call him Jesus. 32 He will be great and will be called the Son of the Most High. The Lord God will give him the throne of his father David, and he will reign over Jacob's descendants forever; his kingdom will never end."

"How will this be," Mary asked the angel, "since I am a virgin?"

The angel answered, "The Holy Spirit will come on you, and the power of the Most High will overshadow you. So the holy one to be born will be called the Son of God. Even Elizabeth your relative is going to have a child in her old age, and she who was said to be unable to conceive is in her sixth month. For no word from God will ever fail."

"I am the Lord's servant," Mary answered. "May your word to me be fulfilled." Then the angel left her.

**Soul Exploration:**

    1.   Do you see yourself as holy and beautiful in God's eyes?

2. What is Christ's call to you through this scripture?



3. What wisdom did He give you? How do you see yourself now? Has He removed something?

# Lectio Divina Day Three

**Luke 1:26-38 (NKJV)** Now in the sixth month the angel Gabriel was sent by God to a city of Galilee named Nazareth, to a virgin betrothed to a man whose name was Joseph, of the house of David. The virgin's name *was* Mary. And having come in, the angel said to her, "Rejoice, highly favored *one,* the Lord *is* with you; blessed *are* you among women!"

But when she saw *him,* she was troubled at his saying, and considered what manner of greeting this was. Then the angel said to her, "Do not be afraid, Mary, for you have found favor with God. And behold, you will conceive in your womb and bring forth a Son and shall call His name JESUS. He will be great and will be called the Son of the Highest; and the Lord God will give Him the throne of His father David. And He will reign over the house of Jacob forever, and of His kingdom there will be no end."

Then Mary said to the angel, "How can this be, since I do not know a man?"

And the angel answered and said to her, "*The* Holy Spirit will come upon you, and the power of the Highest will overshadow you; therefore, also, that Holy One who is to be born will be called the Son of God. Now indeed, Elizabeth your relative has also conceived a son in her old age; and this is now the sixth month for her who was called barren. For with God nothing will be impossible."

Then Mary said, "Behold the maidservant of the Lord! Let it be to me according to your word." And the angel departed from her.

**Soul Exploration:**

1. Do you see yourself as holy and beautiful in God's eyes?

2. What is Christ's call to you through this scripture?

3. What wisdom did He give you? How do you see yourself now? Has He removed something?

# Lectio Divina Day Four

**Luke 1:26-38 (ESV)** In the sixth month the angel Gabriel was sent from God to a city of Galilee named Nazareth, to a virgin betrothed to a man whose name was Joseph, of the house of David. And the virgin's name was Mary. And he came to her and said, "Greetings, O favored one, the Lord is with you!" But she was greatly troubled at the saying and tried to discern what sort of greeting this might be. And the angel said to her, "Do not be afraid, Mary, for you have found favor with God. And behold, you will conceive in your womb and bear a son, and you shall call his name Jesus. He will be great and will be called the Son of the Most High. And the Lord God will give to him the throne of his father David, and he will reign over the house of Jacob forever, and of his kingdom there will be no end."

And Mary said to the angel, "How will this be, since I am a virgin?"

And the angel answered her, "The Holy Spirit will come upon you, and the power of the Most High will overshadow you; therefore, the child to be born will be called holy—the Son of God. And behold, your relative Elizabeth in her old age has also conceived a son, and this is the sixth month with her who was called barren. For nothing will be impossible with God." And Mary said, "Behold, I am the servant of the Lord; let it be to me according to your word." And the angel departed from her.

**Soul Exploration:**

1. Do you see yourself as holy and beautiful in God's eyes?

2. What is Christ's call to you through this scripture?

3. What wisdom did He give you? How do you see yourself now? Has He removed something?

# Lectio Divina Day Five

**Luke 1:26-38 (NLT)** In the sixth month of Elizabeth's pregnancy, God sent the angel Gabriel to Nazareth, a village in Galilee, to a virgin named Mary. She was engaged to be married to a man named Joseph, a descendant of King David. Gabriel appeared to her and said, "Greetings, favored woman! The Lord is with you!"

Confused and disturbed, Mary tried to think what the angel could mean. "Don't be afraid, Mary," the angel told her, "For you have found favor with God! You will conceive and give birth to a son, and you will name him Jesus. He will be very great and will be called the Son of the Most High. The Lord God will give him the throne of his ancestor David. And he will reign over Israel forever; his Kingdom will never end!"
Mary asked the angel, "But how can this happen? I am a virgin."

The angel replied, "The Holy Spirit will come upon you, and the power of the Most High will overshadow you. So the baby to be born will be holy, and he will be called the Son of God. What's more, your relative Elizabeth has become pregnant in her old age! People used to say she was barren, but she has conceived a son and is now in her sixth month. For the word of God will never fail."

Mary responded, "I am the Lord's servant. May everything you have said about me come true." And then the angel left her.

**Soul Exploration:**

1. Do you see yourself as holy and beautiful in God's eyes?

2. What is Christ's call to you through this scripture?

3. What wisdom did He give you? How do you see yourself now? Has He removed something?

# Lectio Divina Day Six

**Luke 1:26-38 (MSG)** In the sixth month of Elizabeth's pregnancy, God sent the angel Gabriel to the Galilean village of Nazareth to a virgin engaged to be married to a man descended from David. His name was Joseph, and the virgin's name, Mary. Upon entering, Gabriel greeted her: "Good morning! You're beautiful with God's beauty, beautiful inside and out! God be with you." She was thoroughly shaken, wondering what was behind a greeting like that. But the angel assured her, "Mary, you have nothing to fear. God has a surprise for you: You will become pregnant and give birth to a son and call his name Jesus.
He will be great, be called 'Son of the Highest.' The Lord God will give him the throne of his father David;
He will rule Jacob's house forever— no end, ever, to his kingdom."

Mary said to the angel, "But how? I've never slept with a man."

The angel answered, The Holy Spirit will come upon you, the power of the Highest hover over you;
Therefore, the child you bring to birth will be called Holy, Son of God. "And did you know that your cousin Elizabeth conceived a son, old as she is? Everyone called her barren, and here she is six months pregnant! Nothing, you see, is impossible with God."

And Mary said, "Yes, I see it all now: I'm the Lord's maid, ready to serve. Let it be with me just as you say.
Then the angel left her.

**Soul Exploration:**

1. Do you see yourself as holy and beautiful in God's eyes?

2. What is Christ's call to you through this scripture?

3. What wisdom did He give you? How do you see yourself now? Has He removed something?

# Lectio Divina Day Seven

**Luke 1:26-38 (NASB)** Now in the sixth month the angel Gabriel was sent from God to a city in Galilee called Nazareth, to a virgin engaged to a man whose name was Joseph, of the descendants of David; and the virgin's name was Mary. And coming in, he said to her, "Greetings, favored one! The Lord *is* with you." But she was very perplexed at *this* statement and kept pondering what kind of salutation this was. The angel said to her, "Do not be afraid, Mary; for you have found favor with God. And behold, you will conceive in your womb and bear a son, and you shall name Him Jesus. He will be great and will be called the Son of the Most High; and the Lord God will give Him the throne of His father David; and He will reign over the house of Jacob forever, and His kingdom will have no end."

Mary said to the angel, "How can this be, since I am a virgin?"

The angel answered and said to her, "The Holy Spirit will come upon you, and the power of the Most High will overshadow you; and for that reason the holy Child shall be called the Son of God. And behold, even your relative Elizabeth has also conceived a son in her old age; and she who was called barren is now in her sixth month. For nothing will be impossible with God." And Mary said, "Behold, the bondslave of the Lord; may it be done to me according to your word." And the angel departed from her.

**Soul Exploration:**

1. Do you see yourself as holy and beautiful in God's eyes?

2. What is Christ's call to you through this scripture?

3. What wisdom did He give you? How do you see yourself now? Has He removed something?

# Weekly Sacred Examen

## A Weekly Reflection

St. Ignatius Loyola's Examen is an opportunity for peaceful reflective prayer. It invites us to find the movement of God in all the people and events of our life. The Examen is simply a set of introspective prompts for you to follow or adapt to your own character and spirit.

Begin with a pause and a slow, deep breath or two; become aware that you are in the presence of a Holy and Beautiful God.

## Thanksgiving

What am I especially grateful for in the past week? (The gift of another day...The love and support I have received...Something I have enjoyed....A moment I felt God's presence.....)

## Petition

I am about to reflect upon my week of Lectio Divina. I ask for the wisdom to know God and to know myself as God sees me.

## Review

What did I learn in the Scriptures I read?

Where did I experience joy?

What troubled me?

What challenged me?

Did I pause and find Selah?

What was something beautiful or holy that was revealed to me?

## Response

In response to this examen of my life, how have I grown my faith? How did I cultivate a place of joy and rest? What did God teach me in His Word?

## A Look Forward

As I look forward, what comes to mind?

How do I want to enter tomorrow? How will I cultivate peace in my life?

## Love | Proverbs 10:12

*Father let me hear from you. Fill my heart, soul, and mind with your presence and discernment from your Holy Spirit. Let your words be a living water quenching my thirst for your goodness.*

# Intro to the Scripture

A key principle in Biblical ethics, seeking revenge never ends well. It only multiplies anger and escalates a negative cycle of retaliation. Choosing a response that is deeply set in love is far more powerful. When we despise each other, we seek to hurt each other. Hatred enters and division follows. When we choose love, we are not choosing to cover up the sin, rather it seeks to find common ground so that we can work together in peace and continue to experience joy.

**REMEMBER:**

**Read** slowly and prayerfully /Lectio (Read)

**Reflect** /Meditatio (Focus on a word or phrase/listen)

**Respond/** Oratio (Pray to God)

**Rest/**Contemplate/ Contemplatio (Rest in God)

**Resolve/**Incarnatio (Carry this Word in your life)

Sit quietly for a moment. Take a deep breath in and release. Allow His presence to wash over you.
Begin.

# Lectio Divina Day One

**Proverbs 10:12 (TPT)** Hatred keeps old quarrels alive, but love draws a veil over every insult and finds a way to make sin disappear.

**Soul Exploration:**

1. Do you see yourself as holy and beautiful in God's eyes?

2. What is Christ's call to you through this scripture?

3. What wisdom did He give you? How do you see yourself now? Has He removed something?

# Lectio Divina Day Two

**Proverbs 10:12 (VOICE)** Hatred fuels dissension, but love calms all rebellions.

**Soul Exploration:**

1. Do you see yourself as holy and beautiful in God's eyes?

2. What is Christ's call to you through this scripture?

3. What wisdom did He give you? How do you see yourself now? Has He removed something?

# Lectio Divina Day Three

**Proverbs 10:12 (NRSVCE)** Hatred stirs up strife, but love covers all offenses.

### Soul Exploration:

1. Do you see yourself as holy and beautiful in God's eyes?

2. What is Christ's call to you through this scripture?

3. What wisdom did He give you? How do you see yourself now? Has He removed something?

# Lectio Divina Day Four

**Proverbs 10:12 (CEB)** Hate stirs up conflict, but love covers all offenses.

**Soul Exploration:**

1. Do you see yourself as holy and beautiful in God's eyes?

2. What is Christ's call to you through this scripture?

3. What wisdom did He give you? How do you see yourself now? Has He removed something?

# Lectio Divina Day Five

**Proverbs 10:12 (AMP)** Hatred stirs up strife, but love covers *and* overwhelms all transgressions [forgiving and overlooking another's faults].

**Soul Exploration:**

1. Do you see yourself as holy and beautiful in God's eyes?

2. What is Christ's call to you through this scripture?

3. What wisdom did He give you? How do you see yourself now? Has He removed something?

# Lectio Divina Day Six

**Proverbs 10:12 (KJV)** Hatred stirreth up strifes, but love covereth all sins.

**Soul Exploration:**

1. Do you see yourself as holy and beautiful in God's eyes?

2. What is Christ's call to you through this scripture?

3. What wisdom did He give you? How do you see yourself now? Has He removed something?

# Lectio Divina Day Seven

**Proverbs 10:12 (EXB)** Hatred stirs up trouble [conflict; fights], but love forgives [covers] all wrongs.

**Soul Exploration:**

1. Do you see yourself as holy and beautiful in God's eyes?

2. What is Christ's call to you through this scripture?

3. What wisdom did He give you? How do you see yourself now? Has He removed something?

# Weekly Sacred Examen

## A Weekly Reflection

St. Ignatius Loyola's Examen is an opportunity for peaceful reflective prayer. It invites us to find the movement of God in all the people and events of our life. The Examen is simply a set of introspective prompts for you to follow or adapt to your own character and spirit.

Begin with a pause and a slow, deep breath or two; become aware that you are in the presence of a Holy and Beautiful God.

## Thanksgiving

What am I especially grateful for in the past week? (The gift of another day...The love and support I have received...Something I have enjoyed....A moment I felt God's presence.....)

## Petition

I am about to reflect upon my week of Lectio Divina. I ask for the wisdom to know God and to know myself as God sees me.

## Review

What did I learn in the Scriptures I read?

Where did I experience joy?

What troubled me?

What challenged me?

Did I pause and find Selah?

What was something beautiful or holy that was revealed to me?

## Response

In response to this examen of my life, how have I grown my faith? How did I cultivate a place of joy and rest? What did God teach me in His Word?

## A Look Forward

As I look forward, what comes to mind?

How do I want to enter tomorrow? How will I cultivate peace in my life?

## Joy | Romans 12:12

*Father let me hear from you. Fill my heart, soul, and mind with your presence and discernment from your Holy Spirit. Let your words be a living water quenching my thirst for your goodness.*

# Intro to the Scripture:

We have hope in Christ, and in that hope our hearts should consistently be full of joy. Even when we have troubles, through patience, we can continue without giving up. Prayer is essential and should be done in every situation because we know God hears us and answers us. May our hearts remain joyous through our hope in Christ. May our patience remain steadfast through our faith and may we always reach out and speak to our Father in every circumstance.

**REMEMBER:**

**Read** slowly and prayerfully /Lectio (Read)

**Reflect** /Meditatio (Focus on a word or phrase/listen)

**Respond/** Oratio (Pray to God)

**Rest**/Contemplate/ Contemplatio (Rest in God)

**Resolve**/Incarnatio (Carry this Word in your life)

Sit quietly for a moment. Take a deep breath in and release. Allow His presence to wash over you.
Begin.

# Lectio Divina Day One

**Romans 12:12 (EXB)** Be joyful because you have hope [Rejoice in hope]. Be patient [Endure] when trouble comes [in suffering/tribulation], and pray at all times [faithfully; with persistence/perseverance].

**Soul Exploration:**

1. Do you see yourself as holy and beautiful in God's eyes?

2. What is Christ's call to you through this scripture?

3. What wisdom did He give you? How do you see yourself now? Has He removed something?

# Lectio Divina Day Two

**Romans 12:12 (AMP)** *Constantly* rejoicing in hope [because of our confidence in Christ], steadfast *and* patient in distress, devoted to prayer [continually seeking wisdom, guidance, and strength].

**Soul Exploration:**

1. Do you see yourself as holy and beautiful in God's eyes?

2. What is Christ's call to you through this scripture?

3. What wisdom did He give you? How do you see yourself now? Has He removed something?

# Lectio Divina Day Three

**Romans 12:12 (NRSVCE)** Rejoice in hope, be patient in suffering, persevere in prayer.

**Soul Exploration:**

1. Do you see yourself as holy and beautiful in God's eyes?

2. What is Christ's call to you through this scripture?

3. What wisdom did He give you? How do you see yourself now? Has He removed something?

# Lectio Divina Day Four

**Romans 12:12 (MSG)** Don't burn out; keep yourselves fueled and aflame. Be alert servants of the Master, cheerfully expectant. Don't quit in hard times; pray all the harder. Help needy Christians; be inventive in hospitality.

**Soul Exploration:**

1. Do you see yourself as holy and beautiful in God's eyes?

2. What is Christ's call to you through this scripture?

3. What wisdom did He give you? How do you see yourself now? Has He removed something?

# Lectio Divina Day Five

**Romans 12:12 (KJV)** Rejoicing in hope; patient in tribulation; continuing instant in prayer.

**Soul Exploration:**

1.  Do you see yourself as holy and beautiful in God's eyes?

2.  What is Christ's call to you through this scripture?

3.  What wisdom did He give you? How do you see yourself now? Has He removed something?

# Lectio Divina Day Six

**Romans 12:12 (ESV)** Rejoice in hope, be patient in tribulation, be constant in prayer.

**Soul Exploration:**

1. Do you see yourself as holy and beautiful in God's eyes?

2. What is Christ's call to you through this scripture?

3. What wisdom did He give you? How do you see yourself now? Has He removed something?

# Lectio Divina Day Seven

**Romans 12:12 (TPT)** Let this hope burst forth within you, releasing a continual joy. Don't give up in a time of trouble, but commune with God at all times.

**Soul Exploration:**

1.  Do you see yourself as holy and beautiful in God's eyes?

2.  What is Christ's call to you through this scripture?

3.  What wisdom did He give you? How do you see yourself now? Has He removed something?

# Weekly Sacred Examen

## A Weekly Reflection

St. Ignatius Loyola's Examen is an opportunity for peaceful reflective prayer. It invites us to find the movement of God in all the people and events of our life. The Examen is simply a set of introspective prompts for you to follow or adapt to your own character and spirit.

Begin with a pause and a slow, deep breath or two; become aware that you are in the presence of a Holy and Beautiful God.

## Thanksgiving

What am I especially grateful for in the past week? (The gift of another day...The love and support I have received...Something I have enjoyed....A moment I felt God's presence.....)

## Petition

I am about to reflect upon my week of Lectio Divina. I ask for the wisdom to know God and to know myself as God sees me.

**Review**

What did I learn in the Scriptures I read?

Where did I experience joy?

What troubled me?

What challenged me?

Did I pause and find Selah?

What was something beautiful or holy that was revealed to me?

**Response**

In response to this examen of my life, how have I grown my faith? How did I cultivate a place of joy and rest? What did God teach me in His Word?

**A Look Forward**

As I look forward, what comes to mind?

How do I want to enter tomorrow? How will I cultivate peace in my life?

## Making Things New | Isaiah 43:18-19

*Father let me hear from you. Fill my heart, soul, and mind with your presence and discernment from your Holy Spirit. Let your words be a living water quenching my thirst for your goodness.*

# Intro to the Scripture

In these verses we see God telling Isaiah to receive His forgiveness and look to our future. Our past is simply our past. We are beings in need of forgiveness, and our Father is more than happy to forgive when we ask, learn from our mistakes, make amends if needed, and then look forward to the new things God will do in our lives. This scripture is the key to letting go and moving forward: accept forgiveness, don't hold onto the past, and look forward to the future.

**REMEMBER:**

**Read** slowly and prayerfully /Lectio (Read)

**Reflect** /Meditatio (Focus on a word or phrase/listen)

**Respond/** Oratio (Pray to God)

**Rest/**Contemplate/ Contemplatio (Rest in God)

**Resolve/**Incarnatio (Carry this Word in your life)

Sit quietly for a moment. Take a deep breath in and release. Allow His presence to wash over you.
Begin.

# Lectio Divina Day One

**Isaiah 43:18-19 (TPT)** Stop dwelling on the past. Don't even remember these former things. I am doing something brand new, *something unheard of.* Even now it sprouts and grows and matures. Don't you perceive it? I will make a way in the wilderness and open up flowing streams in the desert.

**Soul Exploration:**

1. Do you see yourself as holy and beautiful in God's eyes?

2. What is Christ's call to you through this scripture?

3. What wisdom did He give you? How do you see yourself now? Has He removed something?

# Lectio Divina Day Two

**Isaiah 43:18-19 (NIV)** Forget the former things; do not dwell on the past. See, I am doing a new thing! Now it springs up; do you not perceive it? I am making a way in the wilderness and streams in the wasteland.

**Soul Exploration:**

1. Do you see yourself as holy and beautiful in God's eyes?

2. What is Christ's call to you through this scripture?

3. What wisdom did He give you? How do you see yourself now? Has He removed something?

# Lectio Divina Day Three

**Isaiah 43:18-19 (ESV)** Remember not the former things, nor consider the things of old. Behold, I am doing a new thing; now it springs forth, do you not perceive it? I will make a way in the wilderness and rivers in the desert.

**Soul Exploration:**

1. Do you see yourself as holy and beautiful in God's eyes?

2. What is Christ's call to you through this scripture?

3. What wisdom did He give you? How do you see yourself now? Has He removed something?

# Lectio Divina Day Four

**Isaiah 43:18-19 (KJV)** Remember ye not the former things, neither consider the things of old. Behold, I will do a new thing; now it shall spring forth; shall ye not know it? I will even make a way in the wilderness, and rivers in the desert.

**Soul Exploration:**

1.  Do you see yourself as holy and beautiful in God's eyes?

2.  What is Christ's call to you through this scripture?

3.  What wisdom did He give you? How do you see yourself now? Has He removed something?

# Lectio Divina Day Five

**Isaiah 43:18-19 (NASB)** Do not call to mind the former things or ponder things of the past. Behold, I will do something new, now it will spring forth; will you not be aware of it? I will even make a roadway in the wilderness, rivers in the desert.

**Soul Exploration:**

1. Do you see yourself as holy and beautiful in God's eyes?

2. What is Christ's call to you through this scripture?

3. What wisdom did He give you? How do you see yourself now? Has He removed something?

# Lectio Divina Day Six

**Isaiah 43:18-19 (NRSVCE)** Do not remember the former things or consider the things of old. I am about to do a new thing; now it springs forth, do you not perceive it? I will make a way in the wilderness and rivers in the desert.

**Soul Exploration:**

1.  Do you see yourself as holy and beautiful in God's eyes?

2.  What is Christ's call to you through this scripture?

3.  What wisdom did He give you? How do you see yourself now? Has He removed something?

# Lectio Divina Day Seven

**Isaiah 43:18-19 (CSB)** Do not remember the past events; pay no attention to things of old. Look, I am about to do something new; even now it is coming. Do you not see it? Indeed, I will make a way in the wilderness, rivers in the desert.

**Soul Exploration:**

1. Do you see yourself as holy and beautiful in God's eyes?

2. What is Christ's call to you through this scripture?

3. What wisdom did He give you? How do you see yourself now? Has He removed something?

# Weekly Sacred Examen

## A Weekly Reflection

St. Ignatius Loyola's Examen is an opportunity for peaceful reflective prayer. It invites us to find the movement of God in all the people and events of our life. The Examen is simply a set of introspective prompts for you to follow or adapt to your own character and spirit.

Begin with a pause and a slow, deep breath or two; become aware that you are in the presence of a Holy and Beautiful God.

## Thanksgiving

What am I especially grateful for in the past week? (The gift of another day...The love and support I have received...Something I have enjoyed....A moment I felt God's presence.....)

## Petition

I am about to reflect upon my week of Lectio Divina. I ask for the wisdom to know God and to know myself as God sees me.

## Review

What did I learn in the Scriptures I read?

Where did I experience joy?

What troubled me?

What challenged me?

Did I pause and find Selah?

What was something beautiful or holy that was revealed to me?

## Response

In response to this examen of my life, how have I grown my faith? How did I cultivate a place of joy and rest? What did God teach me in His Word?

## A Look Forward

As I look forward, what comes to mind?

How do I want to enter tomorrow? How will I cultivate peace in my life?

# PERSONAL REFLECTIONS

# About the authors:

Jennifer Howard was born in Singapore and has been a dental health professional for the last twenty-five years. She has been married to her husband Erik for twenty-five years, and they have three children, Jackson, Katie, and Keaton. Sharing Christ with others is a true passion of hers, as is encouraging others to live out their purpose in Him. She considers herself a free spirit and has a heart for all people. She loves to lead others in forming an authentic Christian community. Jennifer had the deep honor and privilege of being the Directress of the Junior Daughters of the King Ministry in Marshall, Texas, for ten years, leading young girls and women into a closer relationship with Jesus through prayer, service, and evangelism. Jennifer has an Associate's degree in Applied Science, a Bachelor's in Interdisciplinary Studies, and a Master's degree in Christian Ministry and Discipleship from Liberty University. She is also a 500-hour Master Certified Holy Yoga instructor with the international ministry of Holy Yoga. Jennifer founded the Holy Beautiful Ministry for women seven years ago to bring the Word of God to women all over the world. She strives to bring health to women in body, mind, and spirit. Jennifer loves to give women sacred tools and a sacred space to grow closer to Jesus. Jennifer sees herself as a connector, bringing women together to foster Christian relationships. Her dream is to make our world a more holy beautiful place for everyone. Her love for Lectio Divina was deepened during her studies as a Benedictine Oblate at Belmont Abbey in North Carolina. After living in Texas for over twenty years, Jennifer is now currently calling the beautiful and scenic area of Virginia home. She is passionate about antiques, gardening, and cooking and loves to travel.

*"Now is the time to remember that all you do is sacred."- Hafiz*

Jane Hanna Stoudt was born to two artists in the Texas Hill Country. She is married to her husband Jerome and together they have nine children. Jane grew up in the country and enjoyed spending her time outdoors with her horses and many other farm animals, some of which were quite unconventional: a brown bear, a pet owl, and a lion. It was in her love of nature and God's creations that Jane developed her love of contemplative living and led her to begin the journey to becoming a Benedictine Oblate. A lover of God's word since childhood, Jane began studying and writing about biblical living in 2003 and has continued to share her joys, sorrows, and lessons learned as she walks with Christ. It is through Jane's writing that she encourages other believers to stay on the path and draw close to the Father in close relationship. Jane attended Liberty University and studied Psychology, Religion, and Christian Counseling. Her lifelong passion has always been to encourage women to seek and live in the grace of our Heavenly Father in all they do. Jane has worked with many women as a Christian Counselor and has now retired to follow her calling as an author, artist, and retreat master specializing in Catholic retreats for healing, creativity, and spiritual growth. She is a member and is certified by the AACC in Caring for People God's Way, Caring for Kids God's Way, Marriage and Family, and Empowering Women. Jane calls South Dakota home where she enjoys painting and spending her days in quiet contemplation.

Manufactured by Amazon.ca
Bolton, ON

44238520R00116